IN BETWEEN TRAINS

A God Mission

Yevette Fisher

In Between Trains: A God Mission
Copyright 2024

GLOBE SHAKERS, LLC
GLOBESHAKERS.COM

ISBN 978-1-965553-10-7

This book or any parts thereof may not be reproduced in any form, or transmitted by any means; electronic, mechanical, photocopy, recording or otherwise is not permitted without prior written permission of the author.

All rights reserved
Printed in the United States of America

Table of Contents

Ordered Steps	1
Divine Assignment	8
A Godly Pit-Stop	21
A Healing Journey	25
3 Fold Cord Reunion	31
An Abrupt Interruption	39
Minister the Word Til All Have Heard	43

Ordered Steps

On Wednesday, July 29, 2009, while walking through Kenneth Hahn State Park in Los Angeles, the Lord placed it on my heart to call my cousin Bernadette, who worked at Amtrak in Los Angeles. Years earlier, God had used me to share the gospel with her, leading to her salvation .

When she answered, she exclaimed, "Hey Yevette! I was just thinking about you! What made you call?"

In Between Trains

"The Lord," I replied. "You suddenly dropped into my spirit."

As we caught up, she mentioned that my friend Sherilyn had just arrived at Union Station. After we hung up, I called Sherilyn, but she didn't answer, so I left a message. About 30 minutes later, she returned my call while I was still walking in the park.

Sherilyn asked if I was going to noon Bible study at my church, Peace Apostolic. She explained that she was in Los Angeles for a few hours "in between trains" before heading back to the Bay Area that evening. We were thrilled to reconnect since it had been about a year.

I had originally planned to attend the evening Bible study but told Sherilyn, "If you want to go to the noon session, I'll pick you up from the station." She had just returned from Dallas, Texas, where she visited Bishop T.D. Jakes' church.

I left the park, went home to change, and headed to Amtrak Station. When I arrived, Sherilyn was in Bernadette's office, located in the crew base, where train crews check in upon arrival or departure. Having worked at Amtrak from 1978 to 1987, I was familiar with the area. In fact, Sherilyn and I had met over 40 years ago in the Amtrak reservation department.

As I walked into the crew base, I reconnected with old coworkers, some of

In Between Trains

whom had since been saved. In Bernadette's office, I met a woman named Lynn, who was also filled with the Holy Ghost and baptized in Jesus' name.

I also ran into an old acquaintance, Graham, which reminded me of a powerful encounter we had years ago.

Graham had been on his way to Washington, D.C., to visit a sick friend, Conrad, when the Lord led me to share the Acts 2:38 plan of salvation with him. Moved by the Word, he decided to be baptized before his flight. I took him to my church in Inglewood, California, where my pastor, Pastor Swancy, was in his office.

When we arrived, the baptismal pool had been drained, so Pastor Swancy asked Graham to return that evening before his flight. Meanwhile, my church secretary, Sister Aquila, and I took him to the altar, where we prayed and "tarried" with him. As Graham praised God, he began speaking in tongues as the Spirit gave him utterance. That evening, Pastor Swancy baptized him in Jesus' name. Graham left the church like the eunuch in Acts 8, he went on his way rejoicing.

Back to July 29, 2009—after reconnecting with Graham and others at the crew base, I picked up Sherilyn, and we headed to noon Bible class at Peace Apostolic Church. As we arrived, she was warmly

In Between Trains

greeted by familiar faces from her years in Los Angeles.

Before entering the church, I felt the Lord prompt me: *"Pray with Sherilyn before you go in so you stay focused. She's here on divine assignment."* We prayed a short but powerful prayer and stepped into the sanctuary.

After the service, I introduced Sherilyn to my brother Dwight and his wife Denise, who were navigating a difficult season with family challenges. Dwight had recently been restored to the church after 20 years away, and Denise was newly saved. As we sat at the picnic tables in the church parking lot, Sherilyn ministered to Denise with wisdom and grace.

That day was a beautiful reminder of God's perfect timing and His power to orchestrate divine connections for His glory.

In Between Trains

DIVINE ASSIGNMENT

For the next seven days, the Lord moved mightily—confirming that we were truly on a *Divine Assignment.* We walked in full obedience uncertain of what would unfold. What began as a simple walk in the park had become a walk in the Spirit.

Noonday Bible study was so powerful that Sherilyn and I decided to return for the evening session. That night, Pastor

Swancy taught on *"The Conduct of a Christian Pastor."*

It's amazing how God allows our lives to interweave for His purpose and glory. For such a time as this, our paths crossed once again, bringing us together for *Divine Fellowship.*

Earlier that day, Sister Selena had an incident with a sister at noonday Bible study that caused some anxiety. They had previous issues that made things awkward between them, and the enemy created division. Apologies had gone back and forth, yet they never seemed to grow any closer.

In Between Trains

Selena was planning to buy the sister a gift to make amends once again, but the situation only seemed to grow larger with no resolution in sight. I felt caught in the middle since I had a relationship with both of them, and we were all sisters in Christ.

While Selena, Sherilyn, and I were having lunch, the incident from noonday Bible class came up. In His mercy and mindfulness of us, the Lord used Sherilyn to minister to Sister Selena. She gave her the Word of God, and immediately, she was set free from the situation. *It's the anointing that destroys the yoke of bondage.* She had done all she knew to do—and having done all, to stand. It was time to step back and allow God to take the reigns. If we hold no unforgiveness and have truly searched our hearts, then *there is therefore now no condemnation to those who are in Christ Jesus, who walk not after the flesh, but after the Spirit* (Romans 8:1). We gave God the glory for that breakthrough.

As Christians, when we come together, we should be imparting wisdom, healing, and testimonies into each other's lives. Sherilyn and I returned to Wednesday night Bible class. When we got home, we stayed up most of the night talking about the highlights of Bible study and testifying about the goodness of Jesus.

In Between Trains

As it turned out, Sherilyn stayed the night. We had no idea what we were in for... *Wow! Wow! Wow!*

The next morning, Sherilyn contacted a friend of hers—whom I also knew—named Juanita. Sherilyn told Juanita that she was going to be in town for a few days (what was originally supposed to be just a few hours *between trains*) and that they might be able to connect. Juanita mentioned that she was heading to Whittier, California, that evening to lead a Bible study at the home of a former boss. She invited Sherilyn and me to attend.

Being prayerful and mindful of what the Lord had spoken to us, we felt led to go. When we arrived, we rang the doorbell, and a woman answered—her name was Miranda. Sherilyn had met her before, but it was my first time. Miranda used to be Sister Juanita's boss but had since retired. The Lord had laid it on Miranda and her husband Marshal's hearts to be a blessing to Juanita's ministry.

As we walked into the house, Miranda felt led to pray for me. It turns out she already had the Holy Ghost, speaking with other tongues. Inside, three other couples were seated around the dining room table, eagerly waiting to be taught the Word of God. Juanita's husband, Elder Dowry, was also there to support her in the Bible study.

In Between Trains

The woman, Miranda, was such a gracious host. I thought it was so kind of her and her husband to open up their home to the people of God. Juanita mentioned that they had been doing this every week for the past two years. Not only did they provide a place for Bible study, but Miranda also cooked food for the group every week. That night, she had prepared a table full of delicious food, desserts included. It was truly a sweet time of fellowship.

After we ate, Juanita opened the Bible study with prayer and even taught us a song of praise. At one point, Miranda asked Evangelist Sherilyn if she would mind sharing her testimony of how she got saved. I thought it was so fitting that Miranda specifically asked Sherilyn to speak. The group that had gathered was of mixed nationalities, which was significant because one of the couples had been raised Catholic, and Sherilyn herself had converted from Catholicism to Christianity. Her testimony was exactly what they needed to hear. Hallelujah!

Sherilyn expressed how, before she was saved, the idea of the Holy Ghost seemed strange to her. She told the group about a time when she was invited by some coworkers to a friend's house for Bible study. At the close of the study, everyone stood up to pray. Being raised Catholic, she was confused at first. She thought,

In Between Trains

Why is everyone gathering in a circle? Then, as the prayer began, someone started speaking in tongues in a low tone—something unfamiliar to her. She said it seemed as though some kind of presence was controlling the people in the prayer circle. Not knowing what was happening, she became frightened and determined that "it" was not going to take control of her. *LOL! (You'd have to know Sherilyn's personality—she tells the funniest stories!)* Unbeknownst to her, it was the presence of the Lord that was dwelling in the midst of their praise.

Sherilyn proceeded to share how as she stood there, the power of God was present in the room, and suddenly, something shot up her arm. For the first time, she experienced the power of the Holy Ghost. Wow! From that moment on, she had many similar encounters that eventually led her to receive all that God had for her. She later received the Holy Ghost and was baptized in Jesus' Name.

As Sherilyn spoke, the Lord moved in the hearts of the couples, and the presence of God filled the room. It was a powerful and sacred moment. Up until this point, I had remained quiet, simply observing how Juanita conducted the Bible study. At the end of the session, she asked if anyone had a prayer request. As they went around the room, people shared various needs. When it came to me, I took a

In Between Trains

moment to reflect, and then the Lord placed something on my heart.

My request was this: *"That every man, woman, boy, and girl would receive the precious gift of the Holy Ghost."* I also urged that if anyone sitting around the table had not yet received the Holy Ghost, they should seek Him—because Jesus was soon to return, and the Holy Ghost was for them. Then, I posed a question:

"Is there anyone here tonight who desires to receive the Holy Ghost, with the evidence of speaking in tongues?"

For a moment, the room was silent. After we closed out in prayer, a few people approached me with questions about receiving the Holy Ghost. What amazed me the most was that just a few days later, one of the sisters called Sherilyn and me to ask if Miranda's daughter and son-in-law could come to my church to be baptized and receive the Holy Ghost.

How beautiful it was to see the seed had been planted! The Bible says, *"One plants, one waters, but God gives the increase."* To God be the glory!

On Friday, July 31, 2009, Sherilyn and I attended an all-night prayer service at my church, Peace Apostolic. It felt like we were on a divine assignment that week— one that had originally started as just a two-hour layover between trains. *Wow! What a mighty God we serve!*

In Between Trains

We stayed for a few hours, getting refortified in His presence, and then we returned to my house.

A Godly Pit-Stop

Sherilyn had another close friend in Los Angeles, Kenley, whom she had worked with at the Amtrak train company. We called him Brother Ken because he had been filled with the Holy Ghost but had never been baptized in Jesus' name. She had been trying to see him before she left, but they kept missing each other's calls. Finally, they connected, and Ken was overjoyed to hear from us.

In Between Trains

Sherilyn and I went over to his house, and while we were there, Brother Ken shared that he had been deathly ill. He had lost a significant amount of weight, and his condition was grave. After hearing his testimony about his sickness, we told him we were going to pray for him before we left.

Brother Ken then told us about another issue he had been facing. Someone had broken into his house, and he suspected that his previous tenant had something to do with it. The story behind the tenant was unsettling. Ken didn't know this person well before he let him move into his rental property. He had met a so-called prophet who claimed the Lord said, "Let this person move into your back house and help them." Hmm... something didn't sit right with that. The Scripture says, "The blessing of the Lord makes rich and adds no sorrow."

At this point, Sherilyn and I realized that Brother Ken and his entire situation needed immediate intercession. God had heard his prayers and was sending help. We began by praying for him inside the house, laying hands on him and lifting him up in prayer. Then, we went outside, anointed the fence, the hedges, the patio, and walked around the backyard where the tenant had lived, declaring God's protection and praying over his life and property. The power of God surrounded

In Between Trains

us as we made our way to the window where the break-in had occurred. We declared angels to surround the house and protect it.

As it turned out, the person Ken had rented his back house to had caused nothing but grief. The situation had been a heavy burden on him. But in that moment, as we prayed and interceded, the atmosphere shifted, and we knew God was working on his behalf.

A Healing Journey

A sister in Christ named Pastor Gill stopped by my house. She was going through some things in a season of transition.. The pressure of being newly assigned as pastor over her father's church was weighing heavily on her. As we prayed with her, the Lord instructed us to perform a foot-washing ceremony. We humbly anointed her with blessed oil and washed her feet (John 13:1-17).

In Between Trains

Through Sherilyn, the Lord ministered to Pastor Gill concerning her situation. What was supposed to be a brief stop between trains turned into a Holy Ghost excursion.

I marvel at how mindful God is of His people. He is concerned about everything that concerns us. Trust Him—He will answer your prayers.

That Sunday, we attended church at Peace Apostolic for morning service. A friend of mine, Pastor Tawana , and some members of her congregation were there. That evening, we met Pastor Tawana and her congregation at Pastor Gill's evening service. After the night service, one of the sisters, named Agnes, Pastor Gill, and I went out for a late dinner. Sherilyn was tired and drove my car back to my house. While we were at dinner, Sister Agnes ministered to me about marriage. She asked if I had ever considered marrying again.

I was hesitant to even think about that. I was all for supporting others who had a desire to marry, but for me? I was done! All I wanted to do was perfect my ministry, be obedient to God, and complete the work He had called me to do. I couldn't understand why the topic of marriage kept coming up in various conversations. Some tension rose in me, so we changed the subject. My heart was well-guarded—and rightfully so. I had married my husband

In Between Trains

twice and divorced him twice. I'd had my fill of it.

After I got home, Sherilyn and I stayed up talking, as we had become accustomed to doing whenever she visited. Strangely enough, she began ministering to me about marriage, questioning why I didn't want to engage in a relationship again. I told her I had already had my share of marriage, especially considering that I had married my ex-husband twice. Sherilyn sat up straight on the sofa, clearly amazed. She couldn't believe what she was hearing. Her response was, "You mean you never want to get married again?" She was in total disbelief. I was caught off guard. I didn't want to receive it from

Agnes, and I certainly didn't want to have this conversation at 3 a.m. with Sherilyn. Enough was enough!

The following day, Sister Selena called, and somehow, Sherilyn and I found ourselves talking about the marriage situation again. Selena agreed with Sherilyn. Shortly after that, Selena knocked on the door. She and Sherilyn began praying for me. Needless to say, there I was on my living room floor in my PJs, being healed in areas I didn't even know I was hurting. Sometimes we are in such denial that we tuck our feelings deep in the back of our hearts, unwilling to deal with what's really going on. When we refuse to experience something that could

In Between Trains

be an asset, it can cross into rebellion. We must remain open to the orchestration of God. Deliverance is no easy process; it takes a toll on you and demands energy. That moment caught me completely off guard—whew! It wiped me out. God had set me up!

Yevette Fisher

3 Fold Cord Reunion

Sherilyn was preparing to head home and go to the train station when she shared a testimony with me about when Alice got filled with the Holy Ghost at one of their sister's houses, who attended the church they went to back in the 70s, called The Home Assembly. According to Sherilyn, the story went something like this: they were at a Fifth Saturday meeting at one of

In Between Trains

our sister churches, Bethlehem Temple, and Alice made the decision to go down in the name of Jesus (be baptized).

To understand the significance, you'd have to know that the scriptures outline this as the the salvation plan (1 Peter 3:21, Mark 16:15-17, Acts 2:38, Acts 8:12-18, Acts 10:44-48, and Acts 19:1-6). The Apostles' doctrine is the teaching handed down from Jesus to the early church. The new birth is revealed in Acts 2:38, it is through repentance, water baptism in the name of Jesus for the remission of sins, and being filled with the precious gift of the Holy Ghost with the evidence of speaking in other tongues as the Spirit gives utterance.

Sherilyn shared that the power of God and His presence were so strong that when Alice came up out of the water, she was speaking in tongues. The presence of God was so overwhelming that it left such a deep impression on Sherilyn that she never forgot it, as if it had happened just yesterday. As Sherilyn was telling the story, the power of God filled my apartment. Sherilyn began to speak in tongues, I started speaking in tongues, and we were shouting and running all over that little one-bedroom apartment! The anointing rushed in—*swoosh*! At that moment, we both knew God had something more for us.

In Between Trains

We looked at each other without saying a word, and it was clear that Sherilyn was supposed to see Alice before she got on the train to return to the Bay Area. It was settled. The Lord had laid it on Sherilyn's heart to reconnect with her long-time friend Alice before leaving. OMG!

Sherilyn and Alice hadn't been in contact for a while, and God wanted them to reconnect. What was supposed to be a two-hour wait between trains was now a Divine appointment coming to a close. Sherilyn contacted Alice, we gassed up the car, and set off for San Bernardino, California.

Upon arriving at Sister Alice's house, she greeted us with excitement and, as always, with her warm hugs and kisses. She began to share testimonies of what God had done, was doing, and was about to do in her life. We spent the entire day with Alice, and as the day came to a close, we all went to Sizzler's restaurant for dinner. While we fellowshiped and laughed, as we always do when we come together, I believe the Lord wanted Sherilyn and Alice to reunite.

It felt just like old times—we shared the Word, prayed together, ate, and enjoyed good fellowship.

Before we left, Sherilyn said something profound. Over the years, both she and Alice had joined ministries that were other denominations. Alice was attending a

In Between Trains

C.O.G.I.C. church (Church of God in Christ).

The anointing quickened Sherilyn, and she looked over at Alice, speaking sharply under the unction of the Holy Ghost. "The Lord wants you to get back under the umbrella of the Apostolic faith. There's nothing like it. Yevette never left the faith, and I commend her for that. I believe God wants you back under that banner. The Bible says we must worship in Spirit and truth."

Alice knew and recognized the move of the Holy Ghost and could not deny that it was God relaying a message to her. Sherilyn reminded Alice of a church not far from where she was living. Alice had spoken there a few years prior and had already developed a relationship with the pastor.

Before the weekend ended, Sherilyn ministered to my brother and his wife, my daughter, Pastor Dan (a locksmith on the corner of my street), Brother Ken, Sister Alice, Sister Selena, Pastor Gill, and of course, to me. Whew!

Alice quickly obeyed God and joined the church, and the Lord blessed her richly. She was ordained and working as an active minister there. The Lord had blessed her with a beautiful relationship with the pastor and his wife, and it was very fruitful. Since writing this book, Evangelist Alice Shaw has gone on to be

In Between Trains

with the Lord. Thank God for the wisdom shared by Evangelist Sherilyn. To God be the glory!

Yevette Fisher

An Abrupt Interruption

Sherilyn and I had just returned from San Bernardino. She had packed everything and was preparing to head back to the Amtrak station to catch a connection for her train to Sacramento. As we were getting ready to take her luggage downstairs, I received a phone call from my daughter Nichol. Just when Sherilyn thought the assignment was over, I learned that Nichol was downstairs sitting

In Between Trains

in the alley, injured. Her ankle was broken, and she couldn't even stand on it. Sherilyn and I went downstairs, picked her up, and placed her in the back seat of my Honda Accord.

Nichol had been at some woman's house when her girlfriend unexpectedly returned early from out of town. Nichol, who had been living as a lesbian, found herself in a lover's triangle. In a hurry to escape from harm's way, my daughter told me she leaped down half a flight of stairs. She landed on her left ankle and also dislocated her shoulder. Somehow, in a rush of adrenaline and under the influence of cocaine, she managed to drive home on her broken ankle.

After arriving home, she couldn't make it any further than the alley. Sherilyn, a retired Amtrak employee, could travel for free, so she would still make it to her destination. We prayed for Nichol as we continued on to the Amtrak station to drop Sherilyn off. Afterward, I drove Nichol to the hospital to care for her broken ankle.

At the hospital, the injury was so severe that they took Nichol in immediately. While waiting, I started ministering to the other sick people in the waiting room, praying for them and calling upon the name of the Lord. Once Nichol was put in a wheelchair and taken to a private room, they did x-rays and discovered she had broken her

In Between Trains

ankle on both sides. Surgery was needed immediately.

While waiting for Nichol to go into surgery, I had the opportunity to minister to the nurse who came into the room. I shared with her the plan of salvation and let her know how much God loved her. She was deeply appreciative and thanked me for the kind words.

Meanwhile, Sherilyn had been released to catch her train back home. We didn't realize that all these events were about to unfold. I truly thank and praise the Lord for what He did during those seven days of ministry. It's amazing to see what can happen when you yield yourself to the voice of God.

Yevette Fisher

Minister the Word Til All Have Heard

Think about it—I never received a phone call, text, or email from any of those people, but God knew there was a need. He's so concerned about His people that He will send someone to the rescue. God is always looking for those who will obey His voice. It's not always about making arrangements to minister. Not everyone is called to preach behind a pulpit. The world is our pulpit, and the Great Commission is

In Between Trains

to go out into all the world. Sometimes, we just have to move by faith.

As believers, we must always be available and willing to be used by God. We need to stay in a state of readiness so that God's mission can be accomplished. We are His witnesses, His epistles read and seen of all men. Our lives should reflect His love, His grace, and His calling on our hearts to reach others, even in the most unexpected moments. Sometimes, the divine assignments that come our way are not ones we'd schedule for ourselves, but they are the ones that make the greatest impact. When we yield to God's call, we see how He moves in ways we never could have imagined.

In the end, it's not about us; it's about being faithful to His calling. Our obedience to His voice can change lives, just like it did that week. Let us always be ready to serve, to love, and to minister—whether we're behind a pulpit or standing in a hospital waiting room. God will redirect our steps, so we must align ourselves with the movement of the Spirit. He doesn't need us to have everything figured out; He simply asks that we be willing. Our plans are subject to change, as they did "In Between Trains."

www.ingramcontent.com/pod-product-compliance
Lightning Source LLC
Chambersburg PA
CBHW051719040426
42446CB00008B/958